Walk

encouragement for your journey of faith

THE CHURCH OF ENGLAND

St. Alphege St. Helen St. Michael
SOLIHULL PARISH

Presented to

Sue

on your Confirmation

15th May 2011

kevin mayhew

First published in 2004 by

KEVIN MAYHEW LTD
Buxhall, Stowmarket, Suffolk, IP14 3BW
E-mail: info@kevinmayhewltd.com

KINGSGATE PUBLISHING INC
1000 Pannell Street, Suite G, Columbia, MO 65201
E-mail: sales@kingsgatepublishing.com

9 8 7 6 5 4 3 2 1 0

ISBN 1 84417 245 7
Catalogue No. 1500703

Cover design by Jo Balaam
Edited by Katherine Laidler
Typesetting by Louise Selfe
Illustrations by Steve English

Printed and bound in Great Britain

Contents

Introduction

The earliest Christians called their new life of faith 'the Way'. And that's what it was, and is. None of us arrives in the kingdom of God and sits down to take it easy and enjoy the view. Or, if we do, we're soon yanked to our feet, given a push in the right direction and set upon our way – the Way – which we need to travel if we are to become the people we were created to be, fit for an eternity in heaven.

The Way is not always an easy walk and it takes a long time – all the rest of our earthly lives and beyond. It will lead us into all manner of strange lands and unmapped territory. We'll traverse plains and valleys, scale high mountains and pass through lashing storms, dry deserts and deep waters. There'll be hazards and dangers, and wrong turnings to lure us off track.

But there'll also be warm sunshine and gentle winds, cool rain and birdsong and spring flowers, breathtaking views and thrilling adventures. There'll be friends to talk with, to laugh and sing and share various parts of the journey. And there'll be one who shares every part, for Jesus has promised to be with us through all the ups and downs, the rough and the smooth, loving and sustaining, helping us to carry our burdens as we walk the Way.

Chapter 1

Beginning the journey

Setting out

This journey is different.
For one thing, we all start
at different times,
in different places,
different circumstances.
Some are young when we begin,
some old, some in between.
The journey starts
not when we're born
but when we're born again.

Finding the way

This road has no end and no beginning
or none that we can see.
It may be that we stumble on it,
lost in some dark, fearful night.
Or we may catch glimpses
of a path meandering
tantalisingly on and upward,
far beyond our view,
awakening deep longings
to see where it may lead.
Freedom beckons, new beginnings,
old haunts left behind
and promised lands ahead.
Whichever way it comes,

before we know it
we've decided,
taken that step forward.
Now our feet are on the road.

Getting going

Most of us just can't wait.
We take off with a running start
once we feel the road under our feet.
Well, why delay?
We're going places, aren't we?
A whole world's before us!
We're all geared up,
raring to go.

Those who run before they walk
can sometimes come a cropper.
Let's be wise.
Size up the situation,
take travelling advice,
listen,
and consult the guidebook.

A prayer

Thank you, Father,
for calling us to come follow you.
And thank you that you will provide
all that we need for the journey.

Chapter 2

The Guidebook

Travelling directions

God is good.
He does not set us on our way
without a set of travelling directions.
So, we have the Bible,
full of tales of other travellers,
their successes and their failures,
weary trails and happy landings,
mistakes and gains and losses,
tragedies and triumphs on the road.
And we have the one
who is himself the Way.
He walked with joy his own appointed pathway,
not turning to the right or left
but looking always to his journey's end,
its suffering and its triumph.
His name is Jesus.

Travelling light

Setting off on this journey
there's a new lightness.
Gone the heavy loads –
guilt, shame, fear, hopelessness –
taken from our shoulders,
laid on his.

We start the journey light;
the only load we carry
is the one
especially designed for us.
The easy yoke,
the light burden,
placed on our shoulders by our Father,
the only one who knows
exactly the right weight
that we should carry.

Conversations

The traveller said: I'm not sure I want to make
this journey.
His friends said: Think carefully. Don't be rash.
It may be too hard for you.
His enemy said: You'll never make it.
No use even trying.
His Guide said: I will go with you.

The traveller said: The road is hard and I am tired.
His friends said: Take a little rest. It won't matter.
You'll catch up later.
His enemy said: I told you so, didn't I?
Better give up.
His Guide said: My joy will be your strength.

The traveller said: I just can't take one step more.
His friends said: Maybe this journey just wasn't for you after all.
His enemy said: Ha ha! I knew you'd give up!
His Guide said: My grace is sufficient for you, for my strength is made perfect in weakness.

The traveller said: Whatever it takes, I will press on, with the help of my Guide.
His friends said: We're impressed! Maybe we'll join you on the road.
His enemy said, trembling: I'm beaten, then.
His Guide said: I am going before you to prepare a place for you, and you will be with me there.

Going solo

Going solo sometimes seems attractive.
We may feel companions hold us back.
We're going faster than the crowd,
making better progress.
So we strike out on our own,
leaving the rest behind.
It's fine, our pace unhindered
by the slow and dull and ordinary.
Then a danger rears its head.
Trouble lurks in wait round the next bend.
We need a friend –

or several.
Where are they?
Left far behind,
too far to hear our cries.
We're not so self-sufficient after all,
or meant to be.
We need our travelling companions,
they need us,
if we're to reach the journey's end.

Friends for the journey

We are not meant to be alone,
not in our living,
nor our journeying.
Even our God is Three in One,
Father, Son and Holy Spirit,
loving and communing
with each other.

A friend will not judge
but accept us as we are
and love us still.
A friend will share our joys and sadnesses,
laughing and weeping with us.
A friend can tell us difficult home truths,
knowing we will listen, and attend,
though it might hurt.

A friend will not leave us when we falter,
stumbling by the wayside,
but will lift us, help us to go on
until we're stronger.
A friend won't run before, or lag behind,
but stay close by our side,
sharing the way.
A friend will listen,
not be quick to give advice
before it's asked for.
A friend will understand our heart's cries
sometimes better than we understand ourselves.

Encouragement

An encourager is one who gives confidence.
An encourager is positive
and does not dwell on faults and failings
but enables others to go forward.
An encourager will not criticise or judge
but looks for good in every situation.
An encourager will affirm others in their gifts,
rejoicing in their triumphs
and carrying no thoughts of envy.
Encouragers will stop to help a weary wayfarer,
even when it hinders their own journey.
Encouragers will stimulate the lazy,
motivate the idlers,

kick-start those who've fallen by the way.
Encouragers will pass on kind remarks
and not repeat the other kind.
Encouragers will, simply,
give courage.

Forgiveness

What do we do about those
who stop to give us lifts,
say they'll show us short cuts,
offer us lodging for the night
with hot showers and good food
or just their company –
and then
rob us
or point us the wrong way
or go off with our best companion,
leaving us sad and lonely?
It's all right, surely,
to await our chance
to take back what they stole,
make them suffer too – just slightly –
pay them back?
No.
That's not the way for those who walk the Way.
Revenge is seldom sweet, or not for long.
To walk and live, we must forgive,

however much we're hurt.
Then, only then, can we go on,
lightfooted, light in heart.

A prayer

Thank you, God,
for travelling companions and friends for our journey.
Thank you for sorrows made lighter by being shared,
for hilarious laughter,
quiet conversations,
hearts linked in prayer,
deep silences,
shared views from mountaintops,
exchanged ideas,
mingled tears,
a warm comforting hug,
practical help,
and all the myriad blessings of human friendship.
And thank you for yourself,
the Friend who sticks closer than a brother.

Chapter 3

Ups and downs

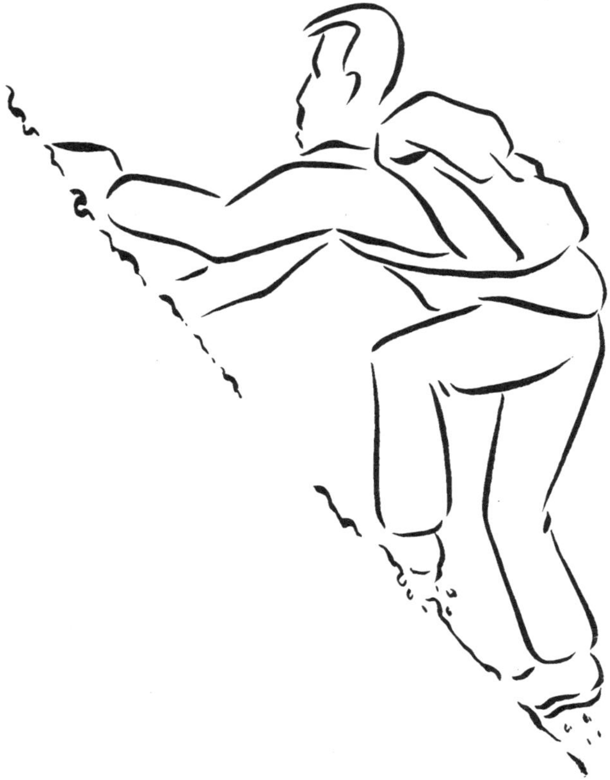

Uncharted territory

It's scary,
coming to a place
you've never been before.
Who knows what lies ahead?
However much you strain your eyes
there's little to be seen.
It's clouded,
dark and frightening.
Will there be hidden dangers?
How will I face up to them?
And will I manage to keep pressing on?

It's not a bad idea
to take a look behind,
remind ourselves of distances already travelled.
It wasn't always easy walking.
Unexpected hazards loomed,
threatening disaster.
But we found we could negotiate them,
even turning them to blessing,
finding, in our weakness,
that our Guide was strong.

So, with confidence
we'll turn back to the unmapped road ahead,
knowing that,
however unexplored our way may be,
our Guide has gone before.

Hitting the pain barrier

A time will come
when it feels impossible to go one step more.
The road's been hard;
an uphill stretch
has taxed each bone and muscle.
Feet are blistered,
legs are aching,
sinews screaming out for rest.
Yet there's the road ahead
and miles to go before a stopping place.
No rest yet.
No choice but to carry on.

A strange thing happens.
Feet that couldn't walk another step
keep going forward.
Flagging joints and muscles keep on moving.
Weariness recedes,
sore places ease,
miles are swallowed up.
Before you realise, you've done it,
broken through the pain barrier.

Fast food

Regular meals are best,
nourishing and well balanced,
whether it's food for the body

or Scripture truths to feed the soul.
Sometimes, though, we need a little extra –
a quick fix, a tasty snack,
food taken on the move,
fast food.
Scripture verses read
and pondered on in leisure moments,
memorised,
can quickly be recalled,
wherever we are,
whatever we're doing,
nutritious and strengthening,
providing, in a time of need,
fast food for the soul.

Two steps forward, one step back

Yesterday I climbed a sand dune.
It was hard work.
Under my feet the ground slid,
shifted, drifted,
trickling down the slope,
making my progress
two steps forward, one step back.
Climbing travellers need to find
a solid place to plant their feet,
a firm base in the word of God.

Excess baggage

How come we started light,
but, suddenly, we're hung about
with all these bits and pieces?
Gradually, they crept in –
a little here, a little there.
Achievements, goods, ambition,
even great ideas –
all good things in themselves –
may all combine
to weigh us down and hold us back.
Excess baggage costs us dear,
needing to be ditched, dumped, jettisoned –
abandoned by the wayside
leaving us lightfooted
and carefree.

One more peak to go

There's one more peak ahead.
It looms above you,
rocky, grey,
outlined against the sky.
You try to visualise the view
from that peak.
What's this?
You've reached it, and . . .
things aren't quite what they seemed.

There's more.
Another peak beyond leads higher,
more rocks to be climbed
before the summit.
And – another . . .
and one more . . .
But then, at last,
you're there.
Breathless and bruised, you made it,
scaled the last stretch,
and now stand tall.
You're on the mountaintop!

View from the top

This view just takes your breath away.
On every side the fields and woods spread out,
blue-misted,
green, gold and brown and green again,
run through by paths,
the silver gleam of water.
The air is clear, the breeze pine-scented,
and, suddenly, mysterious things are plain.
It's possible to make out that puzzling bend,
see why it turned back on itself
to skirt a peaty bog.
And how the path cut through a brambly wood,

avoiding extra miles of moorland.
Now the reason can be seen for that small bridge
crossing at the river's narrowest part.
Standing on this high peak invigorates.
The weariness of miles just falls away.
It was all worth it for this view,
this joyful mountaintop experience.

But the road leads on,
and down again.
It's not so clear this side,
vanishing on rocky slopes,
steep, none too safe.
Who knows where it may lead?
There'll be more mountaintops ahead
after hard climbs.
More views and new perspectives,
wind in hair, pure air.
But now it's back to travelling
down into the next valley.

The Valley of the Shadow

All pass through, some time or other,
sooner or later.
The valley is dark,
it's deep and lonely,
shadowed by loss,

pain and bewilderment.
Try as we may, there's no way to avoid it.
There's no route round, no bypass,
no short cut,
nothing to do but go through.
It's dark,
but we need not fear
the power of this darkness,
for one walks with us,
carrying a stout staff and a sturdy rod
for our safety and comfort.
He'll stay beside us, full of goodness and mercy,
as we come from the shadows
into the light again.

A prayer

Thank you, Lord,
that you're with us in the good times and the bad,
the ups and downs
and varied circumstances of our journey.
We will see many changes as we travel,
and will ourselves be changed by our journeyings,
but you are the God who never changes,
whose love never comes to an end.

Chapter 4

Losing the way

Diversions

Diversions there are in plenty,
waiting to entrap the unwary.
A side-road may come in sight,
looking pleasant and inviting,
beckoning the traveller to try its path.
The traveller pauses,
looking at the road ahead,
rough, stony, the sun beating down.
The way looks hard.
In contrast, the side-road
has sun and dappled shade,
green verges,
and a path that winds softly and gently
round the next bend.
To walk in it would be delightful,
soothing and refreshing,
and the roads would meet again,
most likely, not far on.

Care is needed.
How often do intrepid map-readers
turn off the main road,
thinking that a short cut would be better?
How often do the pleasant side-roads
tail off into impassable cart-tracks
or merely stark dead-ends?
Steps can be retraced.
The way back can be found.

But ground lost takes time to regain.
Diversions may be costly in the end.

Hidden dangers

The worst dangers are the hidden ones,
those you thought never to encounter.
Not just the ones that spring out from the verge
but often those that creep up unexpected.
It's wise to be on guard at all times,
not just in the vulnerable places
but especially when the going's good,
the road is smooth,
the sky blue overhead,
all things set fair,
progress is great.
Beware.
Watch for the hidden dangers.

Pitfalls

Pitfalls are always hidden,
well covered, innocently disguised,
only discernible when our feet are on them
and the ground gives way.

Pitfalls don't advertise themselves.
They often masquerade as something good,
only requiring one small sideways step
to grasp what's offered.

The pitfall maker uses cunning,
playing on weaknesses,
setting the trap with subtly tempting bait,
convincing the unwary that it's good.

Above all else, we travellers need
to keep our thoughts upon our Guide,
eyes fixed on the horizon,
feet upon the road.

Losing the way

However much we mean to keep on course
there may be times
when we will lose the way.
Suddenly,
we find we've taken a wrong turning.
This is not the road at all,
and, what's more alarming,
we just don't know
how to get back.

Don't panic.
Stop.

Wait.
Listen.
Your guide is there
and you're not lost to him.
Very soon you'll hear a voice behind you
saying, 'I'm here. Be still. This is the way.
Now walk in it.'

The foolish and the wise

The Foolish Traveller said:

I am young and strong and fit. I can manage without much help from my Guide.

The Wise Traveller said:

I'm a bit unsure. I've learned I don't really know it all. I need to consult my Guide at every turn.

The Foolish Traveller said:

Everything's going fine. I'm doing really well on this journey.

The Wise Traveller said:

With my Guide's help, and despite my mistakes, I am keeping on the track.

The Foolish Traveller said:
Help! I am in trouble. I don't quite know where to find my Guide, and I'm not sure I even remember his voice.

The Wise Traveller said:
Help! I am in trouble, and I am so glad that my Guide is right here beside me to help me through it.

The Foolish Traveller said:
Phew! That was close. I've lost some ground now and I'll have to work hard to make it up.

The Wise Traveller said:
Thank you, Lord. And please help me to stay close beside you for the rest of the way.

A prayer

Lord, we are so glad that,
however we may wander from the pathway,
we are never lost to you.
Thank you that you will patiently search
until we are found again,
set on the road
and pointed in the right direction.

Chapter 5

Changing scenery

Desert places

The desert is a dry place,
so dry, my tongue sticks to my mouth.
I long for shade and shelter,
rest, and cool,
and, most of all, for fresh, clear water.

The Rock is there,
even in desert places,
offering shelter, comfort,
shade at noon
and streams of living water.

Times and seasons

It's not all hardship, this long journey.
Rewards wait for us that travel.
How else would we observe the changing seasons,
watch the uncurling fronds of fern in spring,
hear the liquid melody of a blackbird
perched high in a tall pink-budded sycamore?
Or feel the summer sunshine warm across our
  shoulders,
smell the elusive fragrance of sweet evening
  honeysuckle,
or taste the sharp sweetness of the first wild
  blackberries?

How would we watch the mist rise on September
mornings,
glimpse the gold gleam of stubble in the harvest
fields,
and marvel at the flaming beauty of the autumn
woodland?
How would we feel the chill of wind against our
face,
experience the wonder of a world muffled in white,
and hear the angry roaring of a stream in flood?
All these, with myriad others, enrich and bless
the traveller,
granting a small taste of wonders still to come.

The scenery is ever-changing too.
There'll be flat green fields and soaring mountains,
grassy meadows and rocky shores,
barren deserts, cultivated farmland, boggy marshes,
wide sandy beaches and towering forests,
snow-covered hillsides and dim, steaming jungles,
deep canyons, quiet river banks, prairies and plains,
all of them needing wise negotiation,
changes of pace, equipment, directions –
all freely supplied by the Maker of all things.

Storm clouds up ahead

It's hot and dusty, close and sultry,
wearisome weather.
Overhead, storm clouds gather,
threatening,
ominously black and purple.
Something's coming.

Only fools ignore storm warnings,
thinking themselves tough enough to ride it out.

Wise people look for shelter.
On this road, there's always a place,
even on the barest stretch.
It's there, the Rock, ready to shield us
until the storm is past.

The dark valley

There's a valley so deep
and so dark
that its sides seem unclimbable.
It's called the Valley of Depression.
Those finding themselves there feel trapped.
There's no way out that can be seen,
no hope, no future,
no faint glimmering of light.

Our enemy rejoices
when he sees a traveller go down into this valley,
telling us he's won.
He lies.
Because no darkness is too deep
for him who guides us.
He has gone before,
shedding his light into the blackest pit.
He'll stay beside us, though we may not know it,
lifting us gently, holding us securely,
enabling us to climb again
towards the higher ground.
And later, when the valley's left behind,
we'll find that we have learned,
and gained great riches,
precious treasures of the darkness.

A prayer

Father God, you have planned our journey
through scenery that is wonderful and
  ever-changing.
Thank you for your creation,
for the variety of life
and for the treasure to be found
at every point along the road.

Chapter 6

Rest along the way

Weariness

I'm tired.
Tired of this journey.
Tired of plodding on
and seeming to get nowhere.
Sometimes I think of what I left behind
and wish I'd stayed.
I'm tired of taking wrong turns
and having to find my way back on track.
Tired of the same old stretch
day after day.
The way seems long and hard and dreary.
Weariness makes my eyes heavy.
I have blisters on my feet,
scars and scratches from mishaps.
The straps of my pack dig in,
rubbing my shoulders.
There are boulders in the way each day,
needing to be moved.
The road seems all uphill.
My friends seem out of sorts,
and I'm so tired.

Carrying each other's loads

The Guidebook speaks of
bearing each other's burdens.
It also says that each of us
should carry our own loads.
How can this be?
It can be managed.
Each of us has two hands.
One holds in place the load
upon our back.
The other can reach out
to help support the burden
of the person next to us,
who, in their turn,
reaches out to help their neighbour.

Rest stops

It's not all hard slog.
Our Guide understands our needs.
So there'll be rest stops along the way.
There may be pleasant interludes
in green and leafy places,
splashing fountains,
long, white, sunny beaches
with white-topped waves
breaking on the sand.

There'll be the time and space
to sleep and read,
relax and talk to friends over a well-cooked meal.
Time to explore, sightsee, meet people
and exchange news and views
of their own journeys.
Time to reflect.
Time just to be.

Don't get too comfortable, you're not staying!

But then –
back to the road again.
This journey must be made,
no other way.
There are still miles to go,
new ground to cover,
territories to be won.
So we put on our walking boots,
get to our feet,
shoulder our packs,
wave goodbye,
turn our backs
and hit the road.

Putting one foot before the other

Sometimes it's scary, going forward –
not knowing what's round the next bend.
There could be an obstruction,
so large that it blocks the whole road.
Or a big hole, big enough to fall into
if you're not looking properly.
There could be something nasty
with teeth and claws,
just waiting to attack.
Or a fierce storm might blow up,
soaking and battering you.
Maybe it's just too hazardous
to go on at all.

Maybe, though, this is all in the mind.
Maybe, round the corner, it'll all be clear,
nothing to hinder travelling speed.
Maybe there'll be some delightful surprise
to help you on your way.
You won't know until you get there.
You won't get there if you don't keep going.
You keep going by deciding
to put one foot before the other.

Marking time

Nothing's happening.
Every day it's just the same slow plod.
The scenery doesn't change.
Nobody interesting comes by.
No new places up ahead.
I'm getting nowhere.
This is pointless.

Be encouraged.
None of this is wasted.
Large parts of journeying may be dull,
routine, mundane.
Complaining doesn't help.
Take each day as it comes,
rejoicing in the ordinary.
It's still progress,
even when it only seems like marking time.

Living in the overlap

We travellers have no real country,
not even a world to call our own.
Or, rather, we have two worlds –
the one we journey through
and one to come.
Both of them claim attention,

our love and our loyalty,
but only one will last.
The other will grow old and tired,
dried up, used up, wrinkled, sad.
Some try to save it, clean it up and cling to it –
to no avail.
The road goes on and through,
winding to its destination –
the other land, where, even now,
the traveller's name is known,
his place prepared.
There, wonders will unfold
more than we ever dreamed.
There, our Guide will present us, spotless,
to his Father,
and with joy unspeakable
we'll know the journey's over
and we're home.

The last lap

So we will run with joy
the last stretch of the journey,
leaving behind the rags and tatters
of our worn possessions,
discarding everything
that slows us down,

reaching with all our might
towards the goal.
We're not alone.
A myriad voices cheer us on,
stretching out hands and hearts
to speed us home.

One more frontier lies ahead.
It's dark and fearsome,
but our Guide is there
and even in the darkness
his hand holds us fast.
The pain and struggle, toil and tumult
fall away,
seeming as nothing
when we see his face.

A prayer

Our Father God,
thank you for calling us to take this journey.
Thank you for your Son Jesus
who walks with us.
Thank you for your Holy Spirit
who is our comfort and our strength.
And thank you that you will be there
to welcome us at journey's end.